DESCRIPTIVE WRITING

By Tara McCarthy

S C H O L A S T I C
PROFESSIONAL BOOKS

New York • Toronto • London • Auckland • Sydney

Cover design by Vincent Ceci and Jaime Lucero
Interior design by Vincent Ceci and Drew Hires
Interior illustrations by Drew Hires

ISBN 0-590-20932-9
Copyright © 1998 by Tara McCarthy. All rights reserved.
Printed in the U.S.A.

TABLE OF CONTENTS

TO THE TEACHER

Descriptive writing is that domain of writing that develops images through the use of precise sensory words and phrases, and through devices such as metaphor and the sounds of words. The term *descriptive writing* rightly makes us think of wonderful poetry, of vivid story paragraphs that help us see settings of forests or seascapes or city streets, of passages that show us people acting, speaking, and feeling in ways that make them believable and real to us.

At the same time, descriptive writing is a "maverick" sort of domain that—ideally—appears in other domains as well. In expository writing, we use description to present facts clearly. In narrative writing, we use description to show clearly what is happening, event-by-event. In persuasive writing, we choose strong descriptive words to present and support our opinions.

To use descriptive writing on its own (that paragraph about the forest, that poem about the sea) or as part of another domain (that expository paragraph about the development of a butterfly, that persuasive paragraph about the need for a student after-school recreation program, that autobiographical narrative), students need the following:

- An ever-expanding **vocabulary** that helps students to precisely name events, feelings, and impressions;
- A facility with constructing **comparisons** (metaphor, simile, personification);
- Skills for **unifying** and **focusing** descriptions so that readers can track along with the writer, see in their mind's eye what the writer sees or otherwise senses;
- A wide variety of **activities** that encourage the use of descriptive techniques in writing in various curricular areas and in speaking, acting, listening, and presenting ideas visually.

This book provides strategies you can use and techniques your students can use to foster effective description as it applies to all the writing they'll need to do.

SOME OF THE BOOK'S FEATURES

A Gradual Build-Up

Parts One and Two encourage students to explore and use descriptive words and phrases to write short descriptive passages. Part Three helps students hunker down into fine-line pre-planning and editing of the descriptions they're writing. Part Four presents opportunities for using descriptive-writing techniques across the curriculum. Activities in all four parts lead up to writing a Personal Essay.

Reproducibles for Reference and Going-On

Some of the reproducibles in this book encourage students to compile their own reference lists of descriptive words and phrases, and to use the lists and accompanying activities to expand upon what they've learned through class discussion and practice.

Activities for Students with Various Interests or Modalities

The Additional Activities that conclude each part are designed to appeal to kids who work and think in different modalities. For example, students who are visually oriented can have fun describing a stage-setting. ESL students can learn word-meanings by drawing words to illustrate their meanings. Aural/oral students will enjoy listening for intonations in speech and learning from free-reads.

GENERAL TEACHING SUGGESTIONS

Use Free-Writes and Free-Reads

Not every piece of writing needs to undergo a writing-process sequence. Recall that writers—young and old—learn more about writing from reading their own drafts aloud to an audience than they do from any other process. In a read-aloud setting where the audience refrains from commenting, writers discover on their own the phrases they wish to keep, change, or delete.

Have Students Use Writing Folders

While Portfolios represent what the student considers "best," Folders contain "everything." The purpose for keeping "everything" is that even the barest, most-scribbled description may eventually be the spur that generates an outstanding piece of writing. Supply students with gummed tags for sections in their folders. Example labels: *My Own Feelings*; *Places I Remember*; *Great Phrases From Books I've Read*; *People I Want to Describe*; *Words and Phrases to Describe Anger* (*Happiness*) (*Puzzlement*).

Present Activities in Your Own Way

You may want to move students step-by-step through the four parts of the book. Or, you may decide to use other sequences to adapt to individual students' interests and abilities. For example, super-star students might move immediately from **Metaphor and Simile** in Part One to **Descriptive Writing About Science and Technology** in Part Four. With students who need additional practice in constructing comparisons, you might move from **Metaphor and Simile** to **Describing People** in Part Three.

In general, work the activities in this book into your general plan for helping students become astute observers and reporters of the amazing things there are to sense in their world.

PART ONE

EXPLORING SENSORY IMAGERY

GETTING STARTED

During the days or weeks in which your students are exploring sensory images, make the classroom itself an exploration site. Tell students how you will do this: Each day before school starts, you'll change the room in some way that most students can detect—fairly easily at first and then with more study as the days go by. Students should look or listen (or even sniff!) for the change as they enter the room, then name it when the whole class is together. Examples:

- Change the position or angle of your desk.
- Position window shades in a new way to brighten or darken the room.
- "Scent" the room with a natural aroma likes cloves, apples, or roses.
- Play different kinds of tape-recorded music.
- Hang a familiar map or poster upside down.
- Put a small item such as an autumn leaf or a pinecone on each student's desk.
- Play one of the many available recordings of animal sounds: bird songs, wolf howls, the signals of whales.

Students may want to get involved in setting up these sensory trips. Set up a suggestion box. All suggestions should be signed.

DO YOU SEE WHAT I SEE?

This is an activity that can help each student appreciate the uniqueness of her or his "visual take."

What You'll Need
For each student, a disposable camera and/or sketch pads, pencils and crayons; time for a trip just outside the school or in the immediate neighborhood

Procedure
1. Explain the activity: During the trip, each student snaps photos or makes quick sketches of at least four things that catch her or his eye. Suggest that eye-catchers may be underfoot (rocks, puddles, plants, small animals), at eye level (playground equipment, cars and trucks, people, windows and doors), or high up (cloud formations, birds in flight, tall buildings, planes, uppermost branches of trees).

2. Back in the classroom, provide folders for students who have sketched pictures and have them tuck these folders away for the time being. Deliver students' photos to an overnight photo lab. In the meantime, before looking at their pictures, students list on the chalkboard what caught their eye on the field trip. The list will probably be pretty general. (See examples in **1**, above.) Keep the list.

The Lonely Rock
By: Emily Manino

3. In the next class period, have each student choose his or her three favorite sketches or photos and write and attach brief labels for them. Examples: *Muddy Puddle*, *Plane and Cloud*, *The Open Window*, *Baby in a Carriage*, *The Empty Swing*. Students should sign their name to the label.

4. Group the photos and sketches in general categories. For example, playground scenes; street scenes; pictures of animals, and so on, and show them using an overhead projector according to category. For each category, briefly discuss with the class the likenesses and differences in what caught the eye of the artist/photographer. How does each picture in the category help you see something special about the subject?

WRITE
Have students who have pictured similar subjects, such as windows, work together to write a paragraph that tells about their different views of the subject. Example:

> Jose's window is shiny and bright. Marla's window looks dark because curtains are pulled across it. Eric's window is open, and a woman is looking out of it.

6. Under category headings, display the photos/sketches and accompanying paragraphs.

THREE WAYS TO LOOK AT A WINDOW
_____
_____
_____

BIRDS IN DIFFERENT PLACES
_____
_____
_____

FOUR CARS, FOUR VIEWS
_____
_____
_____

WE NOTICE DIFFERENT PEOPLE
_____
_____
_____

SEEING DETAILS

You can use this activity to help students attend to visual details.

What You'll Need
Six ordinary objects that can be placed on a table—examples: a vase, a calendar, a lunchbox, a box of crayons, a book, a glove or mitten, a sheet with which you can cover the display

Procedure
1. Explain the activity: Students will get several five-second glimpses of items on the table. In each glimpse, they must follow the direction you give beforehand. (After each glimpse, cover the display with the sheet, get students' oral responses, uncover the display to allow students to verify responses, then cover the display again as you rearrange it.) Examples:

> **Glimpse One** (Display four of the items.) Directions: You have five seconds. Look at the display before I cover it. Be ready to name the items you saw. (Elicit responses and verify.)

> **Glimpse Two** (Add the two other items to the display.) Directions: Look at the display and tell what items I've added. (Elicit responses and verify.)

> **Glimpse Three** (Remove one or two items from the display.) Directions: Look at the display and tell what items I've taken away. (Elicit responses and verify.)

2. Vary, build, and improvise on the activity according to your students' abilities. Examples:
- Arrange items on left, middle, and right.
- Put some items under the table.
- Have a student add another classroom item to the display.
- Abbreviate observation time to three or four seconds.
- Add a tag or tape to one or more of the items and ask students to identify what's been added.

REMEMBERING VISUAL DETAILS

This is an extension of "Seeing Details."

What You'll Need
A poster, or—for the overhead projector—a photo, that has several major features, such as people, actions, landscape details, colors, and shapes

Procedure
1. Explain the task: Students have 30 seconds to examine the visual. Each student then lists from memory as many details from the picture as possible. (Allow about four minutes for this step.)

2. Students work in groups to compare lists and to make a group master list. Groups share their master list with the class.

3. Show the picture again and encourage students to discuss the accuracy and completeness of their lists.

4. Point out some real-life occasions when we get just a quick look at something that we wish we had more time to study: when we travel in a car, bus, train; when something moves quickly past us as we stand still: a bird in flight, a firetruck, a parade. Discuss why "Look close, look fast!/It may not last!" is a good slogan for writers.

WRITE
Ask each student to write a paragraph describing the scene in the picture. For vivid results, encourage use of present-tense verbs.

IT'S IN THE BAG

This activity requires students to describe ordinary objects with great accuracy without actually seeing them.

What You'll Need
Drawing materials for each student; laundry bag containing four or five items that share some similar features such as shape, size, or texture—and sometimes similarities in *use* as well—for example:
- mallet, hammer, gavel, drumstick
- tweezers, pliers, kitchen tongs, hairpin
- lipstick, glue stick, crayon, pencil
- apple, pear, grape, orange, onion
- baseball, tennis ball, Ping-Pong ball, football

Procedure
1. Explain the activity: The "describer" will reach into the bag, and—without looking—select one of the items, determine through touch what it is, and then (here comes the describer's challenge!) describe the item to classmates *without* directly naming it (for example, "baseball") or the specific task in which it's involved (for example, "playing

baseball"). Audience members sketch the item as the describer tells about it.

2. Explain the skills involved: A really-super describer will give such thorough clues about shape, size, texture (and maybe even odor) that the audience will be able to draw the item correctly without ever hearing its name.

A really-super listener will be so attentive to the descriptive details that she or he will draw the item being described.

You may wish to provide a warm-up example:

> This object is about eight inches long. It has two hands or arms on it, which you squeeze together to pull out things. The object is made of metal, and this one has rubber tips at the end of the hands. (pliers)

3. After an item has been described and drawn, take it from the bag and have students check their drawings against it. Which of the describer's words helped artists form a picture of the item in their mind's eye? What details do they think the describer might have added? List students' responses on a chalkboard chart.

Continue the activity: Another describer tells about another of the items remaining in the bag; students check drawings, discuss and chart details.

WRITE

Ask students to refer to the class chart (below) as they independently write a paragraph that compares and contrasts two of the items.

Descriptive Words and Phrases	Item
Round; a fruit; a sort of dimple at one end; smooth; firm; about the size of a softball; smells sweet and fresh; probably red, green, or yellow. Grows on a tree. Often in lunchboxes.	an apple
Round; about the size of a marble; smooth and squishy; probably purple or green; smells sweet *and* bitter; a fruit. I think it grows on a vine. If you had a lot of them, you could make juice. Good lunch snack.	a grape

Apples and grapes are alike because they're both fruits and are round in shape. They also smell much alike, are smooth to the touch, and may both be green in color. However, grapes are much smaller than apples and grow on vines, not trees. Another difference is that apples are firm and grapes are soft.

JUST LOOK AT THOSE SMELLS AND TASTES!

A Little Background: In English, as in most languages, there's not a lot of vocabulary to describe the sense of taste. That's because our taste nerves—used alone—can only discriminate between sweet, salty, sour, and bitter. And even though, on the other hand, our sense of smell can distinguish between thousands of *things* that produce odors, we somehow still have a paucity of words to describe those smells. The words *spicy*, *fruity*, *flowery*, *decaying*, *acidic*, and *burnt* are the ones we mostly use to describe what we sense through smell alone.

So when it comes to describing tastes and smells, we usually rely on general adjectives and adverbs, and on comparisons:

That tastes yukky!   This smells like dog food!

That smells yummy!   This tastes like apples and pears.

Another way to describe smells and tastes is by linking them to our senses of touch, sight, and hearing. Examples:

The smell of roses fell gently over me.   (smell: touch)

The peppery stew nearly blinded me.   (taste: sight)

Her perfume shouted for attention.   (smell: hearing)

The cream melted silkily on my tongue.   (taste: touch)

Blending senses like this is called *synesthesia*. The following activity can help your students recognize and use synesthesia by comparing tastes and smells with colors.

What You'll Need
A color chart or spectrum chart for display

Procedure
1. Explain the task: In a quick-go-around, you'll indicate a color on the chart and call on two or three volunteers to tell what taste or smell the color brings to mind. The faster the response, the better,—and almost anything goes! Enter responses on chart paper, with the color in the last column as shown. You may wish to prime the pump with some examples:

• When I *see* this color, *red*, I think of the *smell of roses*.

• This color, *gray*, reminds me of the *taste of cold oatmeal*.

• To me, this shade of *pale green* is like the *taste of ocean water*.

• The color *pink smells* to me like a *field of wildflowers*.

2. Demonstrate how writers can combine ideas on the chart to come up with interesting images: the red smell of roses; a gray taste, like cold oatmeal; the pale green taste of ocean water; The smell of wildflowers drifted toward me like a pink cloud. Invite students to refer to the chart and supply further images.

SMELL OF:	TASTE OF:	COLOR
mold; lilacs	a sweet sauce; candy	**purple**
wildflowers	pudding; fizzy bubbles	**pink**
roses; a fire	pepper; crackers; salt	**red**
a spring rain; smoke	a lunch you don't like; the tip of a pencil	**blue**
old socks; earth	cold oatmeal; fog, when you open your mouth	**gray**

WRITE

Invite students to choose a color and write a poem or paragraph that tells what the color *is* in terms of tastes and smells (and in terms of sounds and touch as well, if they like).

After students work with a partner to proofread and rehearse an oral reading, they can read their work aloud to a group of classmates. Post poems and paragraphs under the color-spectrum chart and/or ask students to tape-record their readings and take turns borrowing the tapes to play for families at home.

WHAT ARE THE WORDS FOR WHAT I HEAR?

Most of your students probably have very little difficulty identifying the *sources* of sounds, such as a motorcycle, a fire siren, footsteps in the hall, the sigh from someone sad or worried or bored, the speaker who is angry or alarmed or happy. The following activity is designed to provide a vocabulary with which to precisely describe sounds and often the actions that go with them.

What You'll Need
For each student, a copy of the reproducible on page 17.

Procedure
1. Distribute the reproducible. Discuss how the lists are organized and how writers can use them. Provide an example by writing the following sentence on the chalkboard and asking students to replace *said* with the past tense of some other words in the lists—for example *growled*, *mumbled*, *whined*, or *moaned*: "I don't like tomato sandwiches," he said. How does the use of precise words make it easier for the reader to "hear" the speaker?

2. Ask volunteers to use some other words from the list to tell about sounds in precise ways. Examples:

- Ducklings *splashed* in the puddles.
- Skateboards *clattered* on sidewalks.
- He *thudded* along angrily.
- She *flopped* into the chair.

WRITE

Independently or with a partner, students carry out the writing assignment described on the reproducible. Tape-record the paragraphs as students read them to classmates. Students can listen to the tapes later on for review, to get story ideas, or just for fun. Example:

> The slide ahead was slippery. On my sled, I slithered down the slope, down the slinky turns, slicing and scooting.

ALLITERATION

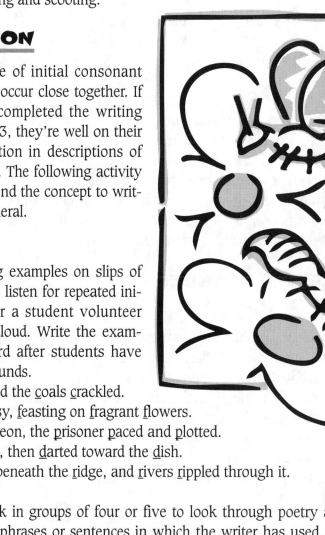

Alliteration is the use of initial consonant sounds in words that occur close together. If your students have completed the writing assignment on page 13, they're well on their way to using alliteration in descriptions of sound and movement. The following activity can help students extend the concept to writing descriptions in general.

Procedure

1. Write the following examples on slips of paper. Ask students to listen for repeated initial sounds as you or a student volunteer reads each example aloud. Write the examples on the chalkboard after students have identified the initial sounds.

- The <u>f</u>ire <u>f</u>lamed and the <u>c</u>oals <u>c</u>rackled.
- The <u>b</u>ees were <u>b</u>usy, <u>f</u>easting on <u>f</u>ragrant <u>f</u>lowers.
- <u>D</u>own in the <u>d</u>ungeon, the <u>p</u>risoner <u>p</u>aced and <u>p</u>lotted.
- The <u>k</u>itten <u>c</u>ringed, then <u>d</u>arted toward the <u>d</u>ish.
- The <u>l</u>and <u>l</u>ay <u>l</u>ow beneath the <u>r</u>idge, and <u>r</u>ivers <u>r</u>ippled through it.

2. Have students work in groups of four or five to look through poetry anthologies and chapter books to find phrases or sentences in which the writer has used alliteration. Ask groups to read some examples to the class.

WRITE

Assign two consonant sounds to each student. Ask students to write alliterative sentences using the sounds. Have students read their sentences aloud.

1. Design Your Own Word List

Distribute the reproducible on page 18. After the class has scanned it to determine what the words represent (sensory images), ask students to list the words in categories that will be helpful to them individually. The obvious categories are the five senses; however, other good possibilities are:

Alphabetize (for reference in alliteration and synesthesia)
Categories (such as pleasant, unpleasant, neutral)
Overused words and underused words

Suggest that students put their lists in their Writer's Notebook to refer to and add to when they're drafting descriptions.

2. A Sensible Trip to the Mall

Ask students to write a paragraph or a poem about sensory impressions experienced at a shopping mall.

3. Chart Starts for Stories

Distribute the reproducible on page 19. Point out that items in the columns can be chosen to create different opening sentences; for example, *The sullen boy strolled into the empty room*. After students have tried out the strategy a couple of times orally, encourage them to add other sensory-imagery to the chart and write their sentences. Discuss ways of using these descriptive sentences as story-starters.

4. Description Clusters

Distribute the reproducible on page 20. Discuss the example to show how the cluster is created: Begin by writing an adjective (descriptive word) in the central circle. Then, in the shaded circles, write nouns to which the adjective applies. In the two circles that branch out from each noun, write two more adjectives that describe that noun. Do not repeat any adjective.

Draw a cluster on the chalkboard and have the class try the activity together, starting with an "easy" adjective such as *soft*, *tall*, *loud*, or *warm*; or a more difficult one such as *purple*, *lumpy*, *bubbly*, or *scratchy*. Then have students work with partners to create clusters, using the form at the bottom of the reproducible.

Students can make a timed pencil-and-paper game out of this activity to play with a group of classmates. Suggest that they use the word lists on pages 17 and 18 for reference.

5. Unusual Homes!

Many younger students may enjoy imagining a land where houses are shaped like flowers, oranges, lunchboxes, envelopes, socks, and other distinctly unhouselike objects. Who might live in them? Have students imagine what these strange homes would look like inside, smell like, and feel like to the touch. Students may want to add details about the sounds inside and out of the houses.

Encourage students to read their stories aloud and/or to illustrate and bind them.

6. Words That Look Like Themselves

The tried-and-true activity of writing words so that they look like what they represent fits right into the context of building a descriptive vocabulary. Because the activity clarifies word meanings, it's especially useful to ESL students.

Name _____

SOME WORDS THAT SOUND LIKE SOUNDS AND ACTIONS

Fast, Light Sounds and Actions

scamper, skitter, scoot,
slide, slip, slither, slink,
sled, slice

Awkward Sounds and Actions

flubber, flounder, flop,
flip, flump, flurry, fling

Unhappy, Angry Sounds and Actions

moan, groan; growl, grump, grouse;
snarl, snort, snicker; wail,
whine, whimper

Sounds of Things Breaking

smash, crash, splash, dash;
clatter, shatter

Deep Sounds and Heavy Actions

thump, thunder, thud; rumble,
grumble, mumble, tumble

Sounds and Actions That End Fast

clip, snip; rap, tap, snap;
crack, smack, thwack

Blowing Sounds and Actions

blab, blubber, blow, blast,
bubble, bluster, burble

Repeated Sounds and Actions

bow-wow, tick-tock, ding-dong,
pitter-patter

WRITE

1. Choose one of the lists above. Write a paragraph using at least four of the list words to describe an event filled with sound and action.

_____

_____

_____

_____

_____

_____

2. Alone or with a partner, revise and proofread your paragraph. Then read it aloud to some classmates. Ask your audience to listen for the sound-action words.

DESIGN A WORD LIST

fragrant	harsh	fragile	velvety	glistening
blinding	bumpy	relaxed	tangy	smoky
shaky	slick	silky	hazy	foggy
chilly	sticky	tense	burning	crisp
sparkling	bitter	choking	bloated	jerky
firm	rough	cool	fresh	heavy
gooey	shadowy	stuffy	warm	dim
sheer	fuzzy	stinging	light	sour

List the words above in categories that can be helpful to you in your writing. Add words to your categories as you come across them in your reading.

1.	2.	3.

CHART STARTS

Choose an item from each column to make three different descriptive openings for stories. Write your openings on the lines below the chart.

sullen	girl	crept	bright	cold	room
frightened	cat	climbed	empty	warm	building
cautious	detective	peered	clammy	disorderly	office
unhappy	boy	fled	dark	musty	house
courageous	doctor	strolled	tremendous	ancient	forest

1. _____
_____
_____
_____

2. _____
_____
_____
_____

3. _____
_____
_____
_____

Choose one of your story-openers. On the other side of this page, add to the story or write some ideas for ways to develop it.

Name _____

DESCRIPTION CLUSTERS

Study and discuss the example:

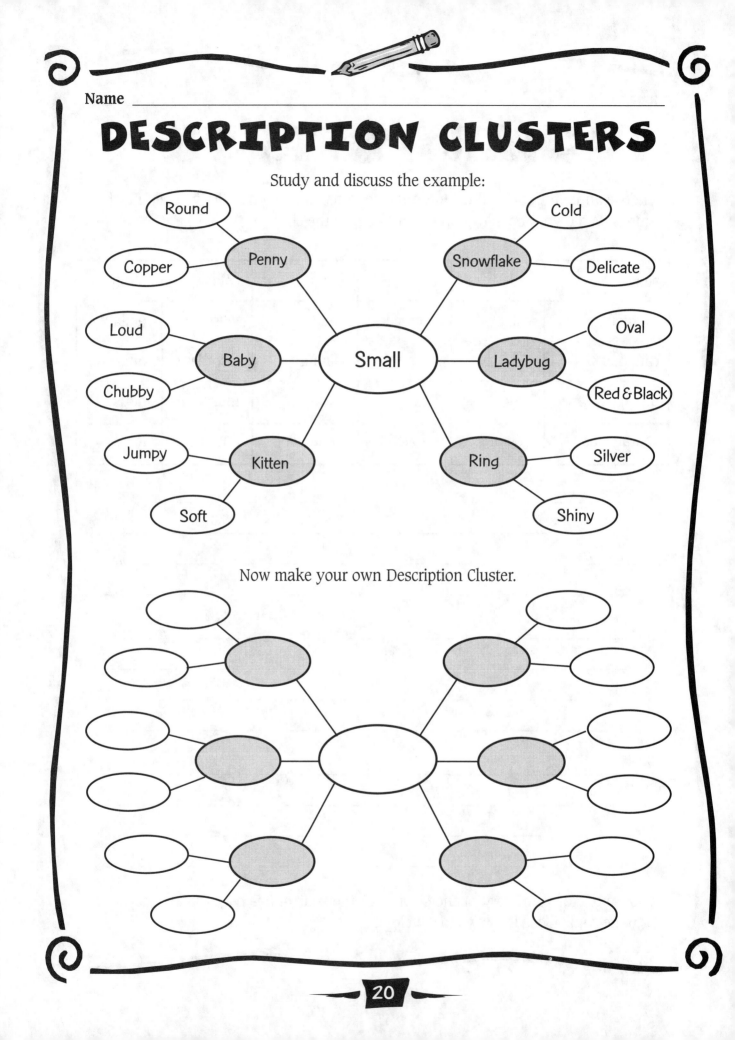

Round
Copper — Penny
Cold
Snowflake — Delicate
Loud
Chubby — Baby — Small — Ladybug — Oval / Red & Black
Jumpy
Soft — Kitten — Ring — Silver / Shiny

Now make your own Description Cluster.

PART TWO

CHOOSING WORDS THAT WORK

Crisp, snappy paper bags, soak in water— turn to rags!

GETTING STARTED

Make words a visible part of your classroom. As your students build their descriptive vocabulary, gradually decorate the room with banners, flags, labels, and posters that present words and phrases in fun, eye-catching ways. You might start by selecting from each student's portfolio or writing folder a particularly fine phrase or sentence, lettering it in color on a long strip of paper and then displaying the strips over the chalkboard or bulletin board. Explain this as the start of the long-range project and have students help you carry the project out. Examples:

- Great lines from poems (including student poems)
- Fine descriptive sentences from books—both fiction and nonfiction— that students are reading
- Powerful antonyms and unusual synonyms
- Words that sound like what they mean

As students complete the activities in this section, they'll think of many ways to wrap their room in words!

CLEANING OUT THE WORD CLOSET

In oral language, students—like almost all of us—use worn-out words from time to time. Some of these ineffective words and expressions are long-standing cliches: "cute as a button," "pretty as a picture," "quiet as a mouse." More frequent among students, however, are the trendy words that seem to be on every student's lips for a year or so, before giving way to a new batch—words like *awesome*, *rad*, *bad* (for good), *mega*, *spastic*; along with the ever-present *awful*, *great*, *ugly*, *wonderful*, etc.

Here's a way to help students recognize and replace tired or trendy expressions with more effective ones in their writing.

Procedure

1. Copy the chart below on a chalkboard. After students read the lists aloud, ask them if they can figure out why the columns are headed as they are. Present sentences that can help them to draw a conclusion. Examples:
   - The Grand Canyon is *awesome*.
   - The Grand Canyon is *striped* with *brilliant* colors.
   - The music was *awful* and *yukky*.
   - The music was *shrill* and *out-of-tune*.
   - She's *funny* and *nice*.
   - She has a quick *sense of humor* and *considers other peoples' feelings*.

OPINION WORDS	FACT WORDS
ugly	misshapen, splotchy
yukky	gooey, sweaty
awesome	snow-covered, steep
awful	shrill, tune-less
great	inspiring, rewarding
funny	humorous, unusual
nice	helpful, considerate
boring	slow-moving, repetitive

Help students notice that the words in the first column, **OPINION WORDS**, simply *tell* what the speaker or writer thinks about a subject; while the words in the second column, **FACT WORDS**, *show* by supplying examples or sensory details.

2. Invite students to recall questions they ask when a friend calls something *boring*, *awesome*, *nice*, and so on: they're likely to ask for facts to support the opinion. For example: "What was boring about it?" "Why was it awesome?" "How was it nice?" Discuss the fact that we can often ask a *speaker* to clarify and give details, but that we can seldom ask a *writer* to do this; writers try to supply the audience with the facts and imagery it needs to grasp an idea or a scene clearly.

3. Encourage students to build the lists. Literature is the best source of additions to list 2. As an away-from-school assignment, students can listen for and note opinion words (TV ads and talk-shows are excellent sources!) and then add them to list 1.

WRITE

Have students make greeting cards with messages that *do not* use opinion words or tired expressions. You might share with them first a few examples of messages that *do* ("To a Great Friend," "Thanks for the Wonderful Gift," and so on). Encourage students to fold their cards in unusual ways, make them of nontraditional sizes or materials, or illustrate them with cut paper and other collage materials.

DEVELOPING CONTRASTS: ANTONYMS

This activity helps students build a vocabulary for describing both subtle and strong differences.

What You'll Need
Copies of the reproducible on page 31

Procedure
1. Start with a brief listening activity. Students are to listen to determine which words in a sentence pair change the imagery.

(Encourage visualization: If students close their eyes while listening, the task will be easier for them.) Though the significant words are underlined below, don't stress them as you read aloud. After students identify the words in each pair, write the antonyms (for example, *glaring*, *soft*) in columns on the chalkboard.
- The *glaring* lights *hit* us.
- The *soft* lights *caressed* us.
- The waves *surged* toward the *sunlit* beach.
- The waves *crept* toward the *dark* beach.
- *Stunted* trees *drooped* along the *narrow* path.
- *Enormous* trees *stretched* along the *wide* path.

2. Discuss the chalkboard list. How did the listed words change the way students saw scenes in their mind's eye? Explain to or remind students that words that have opposite, or almost opposite, meanings are called *antonyms*. You may wish to call out common words such as *big*, *slow*, *happy*, *heavy*, and *ugly* and have students respond with the antonyms.

3. Distribute the reproducible and discuss how the antonym list can help students in their descriptive writing, for example, when they wish to point out how things or events are different. You may wish to add that many antonyms fit only in certain contexts. For instance: a *new* book and an *old* book; but, a *young* person and an *old* person.

WRITE

Ask students to write personality sketches of two television characters from the same or different sitcoms who are quite opposite from one another. Stress **(a)** that the sketches should include many words and phrases that present contrasting images of the characters' appearances, personalities, and typical behavior; **(b)** the sketches are *not* to be summaries of plots or events in the programs.

CHOOSING AMONG SYNONYMS

Through this activity, students develop a strategy for selecting the most precise descriptive word.

What You'll Need
Copies of the reproducible on page 32; several student thesauruses and dictionaries

Procedure
1. Write the following sentences on the chalkboard, words underlined as shown. Distribute the reproducible. Ask students to read each sentence silently, then find a word or phrase on the reproducible that is more precise than the underlined words. Call on students to read their revisions aloud. Keep the activity moving as quickly as possible and accept different responses.

- She was always <u>giving stuff away</u>. (generous, unselfish, big-hearted)
- My coat was <u>real wet</u>. (damp, soggy, soaking, drenched)
- The diamond ring looked <u>great</u>! (perfect, flawless)
- They stared at the ET in <u>a scared way</u>. (horror, shock)
- We'd like him better if he weren't so <u>stuck-up</u>. (vain, conceited, arrogant, egotistical)
- Maybe you were too <u>fast</u> in making that choice. (impulsive, hasty, careless, hurried)
- He had to <u>get</u> behind the tree to avoid the oncoming truck. (dodge, duck, escape)
- I could <u>eat</u> that sandwich in about two seconds! (devour, gobble)
- She's too <u>sort of quiet</u> to read her story aloud. (modest, shy, timid)
- He gave his report card a <u>sad</u> look. (gloomy, somber)
- The lights were so <u>shiny</u> that they hurt my eyes. (bright, dazzling)
- She was whistling a <u>happy</u> tune. (cheerful, merry, lively)

2. Discuss how synonyms are words with *almost* the same meaning, and that writers choose synonyms according to the context of the sentence. Present some examples from the list on the reproducible.
- *bright* lights; *luminous* water; *radiant* sunshine; *gleaming* stars; *glossy* hair; *dazzling* smile
- *liberal* allowance; *unselfish* volunteer; *big-hearted* grandparents; *generous* offer; *lavish* party

3. Have students work with partners or in small groups to find additional synonyms to add to the ones on the reproducible. Then have students refer to *Just a Few Antonyms* (page 31); point out that the words in each column are also synonyms (such as *mute, silent, soundless*; *doubtful, mistrusting, skeptical*).

WRITE

Ask students to write a two-paragraph Personal Sketch telling about two incidents in their life that filled them with two different emotions or to which they reacted differently. In their sketches, students should use precise words that help readers visualize the experiences and how they were different. Encourage use of the word lists students have been constructing and discussing. Suggest the following format (examples are in parentheses):

TITLE:
   (Two Encounters with Clowns)

FIRST PARAGRAPH:
   Start with a topic sentence that summarizes your feelings about or reactions to the first incident. **(The first time I saw a clown, I was panic-stricken!)** Continue with details that describe you and the incident.

SECOND PARAGRAPH:
   Your topic sentence here should be a contrast to the first one. **(In my next clown encounter, my fear vanished, and I collapsed into giggles**.) Continue with details that describe you and the incident, and that show how it was different from the first one.

Invite students to read their paragraphs aloud. Ask the audience to listen for words and phrases that they find particularly vivid and accurate.

METAPHOR AND SIMILE

Many of your students are already familiar with these descriptive strategies. The following activity reviews them and prepares students for using a particular kind of metaphor, *personification*.

What You'll Need
Books and stories your students have been reading; a few poetry anthologies

Procedure
1. Ahead of time, write the following lines on the chalkboard:

The moon's the Northwind's cookie,
He eats it day by day.

The moon was a ghostly galleon* (ship)
Tossed upon stormy seas...

Wind is a cat
That prowls at night...

The fog comes on little cat feet...

My heart is like a singing bird...

...the wind's like a whetted* knife (sharp)

Discuss the images with students. (You may want to introduce the discussion by sharing the old saying: "Poets lie in order to tell the truth.") Are any of these statements factually true? Of course not! Do they help us to sense and see the moon, the wind, the fog, a happy feeling in a new way? What makes all the examples alike? (They compare one thing with another.)

After ascertaining that students can identify the comparisons, review the word *metaphor*: a figure of speech that compares one thing with another. Point out that some metaphors use the words *as* and *like*, as in the last two examples. These metaphors are called *similes*.

2. Play a fast go-round of "Compare." Call on students to quickly come up with a metaphor that states how the one thing is like the other. Encourage some elaboration. Provide an example: **moon - wheel** The moon was (or was like) a bright wheel in the midnight sky.
- truck - lion
- window - eye
- snow - feather
- bed - ship
- cloud - pillow
- lake - mirror
- leaf - page
- smile - sun
- road - ribbon
- hair - waterfall
- music - laughter
- sadness - gray

3. Have students work in groups of four or five. Each group looks through the books and anthologies to find at least five sentences or lines that are examples of metaphor/simile. A group scribe copies each example on a separate sheet of paper and notes the source. Group members illustrate the metaphors. Students can show their work and read it aloud; or make a folder for all the contributions for students to study and enjoy at their leisure.

WRITE

Ask students to use metaphors and other sensory language in factual reports they're drafting for science or social studies. Explain that metaphors often help readers sense and get visual pictures of natural phenomena or historical events. Provide some examples:

- The Revolutionary Army was like a band of tattered, shivering orphans. The British troops were like boastful kids on the playground, showing off their weapons and fancy clothes.

- The rainforest is a house with many levels to it. On the top floor live many animals that never descend to the bottom. On the middle floors live other animals who occasionally go downstairs or go up to mingle with their neighbors.

As partners hold writing conferences, they can suggest where metaphors might be useful and/or check the accuracy of the ones they've used.

PERSONIFICATION

Personification is metaphor in which human characteristics are ascribed to nonhuman things. It's such a common device in writing and speaking that we seldom realize we're using it. (The sun *smiles* down on us. The thunder *threatens* us. The stars *wink*.) In learning to recognize personification, students can become adept in using it in their writing.

What You'll Need

Books and stories your students have been reading; a few poetry anthologies

Procedure

1. Ahead of time, write these poems on the chalkboard:

> The hail falls pitterpat,
> And fiercely rattles down upon
> The brave old pine tree's hat.
>
> -Basho

> The willows hanging low
> Shake from their long and trailing skirts
> The freshly fallen snow.
>
> -Tsuru

Explain the term personification and discuss the images with students. To what are the pine tree and the willow trees compared? (a brave old man wearing a hat; women wearing long skirts) Point out that even the hail is made to seem alive through the word *fiercely*. Students may also recall the first example on page 26, in which the north wind is compared to a person eating a cookie.

2. From your poetry anthologies, read lines from several poems in which personification is used. Example:

> The leaves had a wonderful frolic.
>> They danced to the wind's loud song.
> They whirled, and they floated, and scampered.
>> They circled and flew along.
>
>> (from "The Leaves" —author unknown)

Point out that in many cases, a whole poem may be an example of personification, as when a nonhuman entity actually becomes the speaker, "I." Example:

> I am an oak,
> a mighty tree,
> I grew from an acorn, small;
> with a tiny cap, and a tiny stem—
> who knew I'd grow so tall?
>
>> ("I Am an Oak" by Helen H. Moore)

Invite student partners to find examples of personification in literature the class has been reading. Partners might write the examples, then read them aloud and ask classmates to guess the source.

WRITE

Ask students to choose a nonhuman entity and write a poem, journal entry, or anecdote from the entity's "I" point of view. Preface the activity with these warm-ups:

Brainstorm for possible "speakers."
Have students suggest ordinary objects and animals who might have a story to tell. Write ideas on the chalkboard. Examples:

• a tired pencil	• the school hallway	• the playground at recess
• the family car	• a deserted house	• a lost sock
• a mosquito	• a hurricane	• a frog
• the chalkboard	• a student's desk	• a sandwich

Review some of the descriptive writing strategies students can strive to use.
You might write these examples on the chalkboard or on poster paper for easy reference:

- Use sensory words to describe smells, sounds, tastes, sights, and the way things feel to the touch.
- Use precise fact words rather than opinion words.
- Use antonyms to build sharp contrasts.
- When considering synonyms, choose the one that fits the context best.
- Use metaphor and simile to build images and word pictures.

Also remind students that the word lists they've constructed using the reproducibles are a good source of vivid descriptive vocabulary.

Have partners follow writing process steps to fine-tune their products for this activity. As publishing options, students can consider read-alouds, anthologies, and individual illustrated booklets.

ADDITIONAL ACTIVITIES

1. Being a Book
Distribute the reproducible on page 33. Ask students to imagine that they *are* their favorite book. Using their personification skills, students write about what the book senses and feels about the story between its covers. Suggest that if the "book's report" is vivid enough, the audience will be able to guess its title.

2. Poor Me!
Students can write letters to an Advice Columnist, with the letters coming not from humans, but from animals, things, or phenomena that are experiencing some kind of difficulty. Letters should contain sensory details and vivid descriptions that make the problem clear. Example:

> Dear Solve-It:
>
> I have a lot of trouble making friends, even though I'm lovely to look at (black and white), soft as a cloud to the touch, and wispy-tailed and bright-eyed. My family has told me that I'm rejected because of my occasional odor, yet I've always thought of this as my strongest point! I can send that smell wafting for miles on a strong spring breeze. And that musty, chokey smell is a fine defense against my enemies. Still, I would like to have more friends. What do you advise?
>
> B.A. Skunk

Students might also enjoy responding as Solve-It, with advice for the letter-writer.

3. What Makes It Work?

To see how imagery "works," students can follow these steps:

Choose a short lyric poem or a descriptive paragraph from a favorite book. Copy it, but in place of the sensory words and phrases, draw blank lines to write on.

> I highly recommend myself to you, because_____

Make copies of your copy! Distribute the copies to some classmates. Ask them to write their own descriptive words and phrases in the blanks.

Ask your classmates to read their completed copies aloud. Talk about the different images and feelings. Then read the original poem or passage aloud.

4. Biographical Images

Ask students to select someone they've been studying in your history curriculum and list four or five key incidents in that person's life. Discuss what the person was likely to have sensed and felt during the different incidents. Record students' input on the chalkboard.

Ask each student to choose one of the incidents and write a descriptive paragraph that expresses the historical figure's feelings and sensory observations. Stress that the paragraph's purpose is not to tell about a sequence of events, but rather to focus on the person's *reaction* to the event.

5. "WANTED" Posters and Flyers

Students can make "Wanted" notices for nonhuman entities. The notices—like the real ones displayed in post offices—should give explicit data about what observant citizens should be on the look-out for, and should feature a picture. See example at right.

WANTED: RAINBOW

Wears many colors. Is likely to hang out in the sky but also has been seen in puddles and prisms. Especially likes moist weather. Favorite costume is a huge arc, reaching like a bending bridge from horizon to horizon. Disappears suddenly, fading like a dream! If sighted, notify artists and crayon manufacturers.

Some other possible subjects for "Wanted" posters:

- spring (or any of the other seasons)
- the moon
- a lost sock
- a song to which you've forgotten the words
- a hug
- an icicle
- the smell of pine trees
- the taste of your favorite flavor of ice cream
- a favorite toy that got lost a long time ago

JUST A FEW ANTONYMS

Use this list, and add to it, as you do your descriptive writing.

round, circular →	flat, level, straight
mute, silent, soundless →	roaring, blasting, clattering
glance, peek, glimpse →	stare, gape, gaze
sweet, fragrant, spicy →	fetid, reeking, putrid
rough, coarse, scratchy →	soft, silky, smooth
hurt, ache, painful →	painless, pleasant, comfortable
brilliant, intelligent, wise →	witless, dense, shortsighted
gullible, trusting →	doubtful, mistrusting, skeptical
hazy, fuzzy, faint →	distinct, clear, visible
tasty, flavorful, appetizing →	bitter, offensive, sour
blazing, burning, firey →	cool, icy, chilly
solid, thick, dense →	light, delicate, feathery

Add your own antonyms below:

_____ → _____
_____ → _____
_____ → _____
_____ → _____
_____ → _____
_____ → _____
_____ → _____
_____ → _____
_____ → _____
_____ → _____
_____ → _____
_____ → _____
_____ → _____

JUST A FEW SYNONYMS

Use this list, and add to it, as you do your descriptive writing.

Avoiding Things: → dodge, duck, shun, swerve, flee, escape
_____

Perfect: → flawless, complete, pure, spotless, fresh
_____

Shy: → modest, meek, humble, reserved, timid, coy
_____

Vain: → conceited, arrogant, proud, egotistical
_____

Cheerful: → merry, elated, lively, lighthearted, chipper
_____

Generous: → unselfish, big-hearted, liberal, lavish
_____

Impulsive: → hasty, careless, offhand, hurried, thoughtless
_____

Moist: → damp, soggy, soaking, drenched, saturated
_____

Eating: → devour, gobble, sip, taste, feast, chew
_____

Fear: → alarm, terror, dismay, dread, horror, anxiety
_____

Bright: → luminous, radiant, gleaming, glossy, dazzling
_____

Gloomy: → dreary, shady, dismal, somber, bleak, desolate
_____

BEING A BOOK

Write the title of your favorite book, then "speak" for your book.
Complete the sentences to tell readers what they can expect.

My name is _____
(Title of Book)

1. Here are some of the sounds you'll hear between my covers:

_____

_____

_____

2. I'm full of images. You'll probably like the sight of _____

_____

_____

_____. But the image of _____

_____

_____ may make you feel anxious, sad, or angry.

3. Turn my pages, and get ready to taste _____

_____ , touch _____

_____ , and smell _____

_____ .

4. The characters who live inside me experience many different feelings.
For example, _____ feels _____
(name of character)
when _____

_____ .

_____ feels _____
(name of another character)
when _____

_____ .

5. I highly recommend myself to you, because _____

_____ .

PART THREE

ORGANIZING DESCRIPTIVE PARAGRAPHS

Top

Middle

Bottom

GETTING STARTED

In writing and in formal speaking, *unity* means that all the parts relate to the whole; and *coherence* means that all the parts flow together, fit together, and follow one another in a logical way that readers can understand. Can young writers begin to understand and reach for these classic goals of unity and coherence? Yes, indeed! In fact, students are well on their way to this goal—whether they know it or not—if they've begun to attend to the instructions:

• Stick to the subject. Delete ideas that don't fit. (**Unity**)
• Make sure you give all the steps and details your readers need. (**Coherence**)

Both unity and coherence call for organization. The activities in Part Three show students how to use the descriptive writing techniques they've tried in Parts One and Two to organize unified and coherent paragraphs, stories, and personal sketches.

To establish a classroom atmosphere for this section, you might start each school day by reading a descriptive paragraph or two from a story, nonfiction book, textbook, or periodical feature article that *you* feel has exemplary unity and coherence. Ask students the following questions:

• What does this passage describe?
• What details help you see and sense the main idea or image?

By presenting fine examples each day, you will "wrap" your students in good writing. Each model *you* present and *they* discuss will strengthen students' ability to write descriptive passages.

TOP-TO-BOTTOM, SIDE-TO-SIDE

This activity introduces students to spatial organization in descriptive writing.

What You'll Need
Three or four common household objects (suggested: a broom, a table lamp, a small radio or "boombox", a basket with a handle); copies of the reproducible on page 46.

Procedure
1. In these years around the millennium, time-capsules are in the news. Discuss with students the kinds of things that are stored in these capsules: usually objects that seem quite ordinary to us but that might be puzzling and intriguing to people opening the capsules centuries from now.

Show the objects you've brought as examples (see above). Ask students to imagine that they are seeing them for the first time, and—as careful reporters—are describing them to an intrigued audience of listeners or readers. The objects should be described from top-to-bottom or from side-to-side. Present an example as you hold the broom with the bristles at the top, metal hanger at the bottom. Stress the position words (underlined) as you point.

> This peculiar item is about five feet tall. <u>At the top</u> are hundreds of long bristles, bound about <u>midway</u> with cord. <u>Below</u> the binding, the bristles are attached to a long wooden pole about two inches in diameter. <u>At the bottom</u> of the pole is small metal ring.

Reverse the position of the broom (bristles at the bottom) and call on a volunteer to describe it in this position.

2. Adapt Step 1 above as you describe from left-to-right or from right-to-left the radio or the basket. Again, stress position words (right, left, middle, center, beside, next to, etc.).

WRITE
Distribute the reproducible and preview the lists. Ask partners to refer to and use the list as they draft a description of another of the items you've brought for display, or of another ordinary object in the classroom. The challenge is to describe the object so well that classmates will be able to guess what it is *without* hearing it named explicitly.

After students read a description aloud, ask the audience to tell what details and position words helped them identify the item.

NEAR-TO-FAR, FAR-TO-NEAR

Descriptions organized in these ways require the writer to choose a focus point and then move away from it or toward it.

Procedure

1. Ask students to close their eyes to prepare for a visual trip. Explain that you will describe a scene. In addition to seeing the scene in their mind's eye, students are to decide whether the description takes them from up-close to farther-away, or from far-away to up-close. Slightly stress the underlined words as you read aloud:

> <u>Around</u> you, snow-covered trees hang down over the the path. A few steps <u>ahead</u> is an icy stream, flowing slowly <u>away from</u> you, curling toward the tiny cabin <u>in the distance</u>. <u>Beyond</u> the cabin, hills loom up, their peaks seeming to disappear into the <u>far-away</u> clouds.

Most students will have little difficulty identifying the focus as near-to-far. Ask them to recall the words and phrases that made this focus clear.

2. Adapt Step 1 above. Explain to students that on this far-to-near visual trip, they are to listen for spatial words and phrases and also be able to name the object being described (fire engine).

> The red speck <u>on the horizon</u> gets larger as it moves <u>toward</u> me. Hurrying <u>forward</u> past the park, it clangs and whines with a <u>growing</u> clamor. Now it is <u>halfway</u> up the block, now it is <u>next to</u> me for a moment, passing <u>close</u> enough to deafen me with its noise.

3. Briefly discuss how choosing a visual focus for a description helps the audience see a scene or event clearly. You may wish to reproduce and distribute the visual-trip paragraphs above for students to refer to as examples as they organize their own descriptive paragraphs.

4. Present the following paragraph on the chalkboard. Ask the class to select a focus, then revise the paragraph together to make the focus clear.

> This street changes as you walk along it. Next to my house is an empty lot filled with strong, scraggly weeds and wildflowers. In the distance, I can see two towering office buildings. Just beyond the lot is Mrs. Jimez's news shop. Coming out of my front door, I walk through my mother's sunny flower garden. As I pass the shop, rows of apartments line the street.

Sample revision:

> This street changes as you walk along it. Coming out of my front door, I walk through my mother's sunny flower garden. Next to my house is an empty lot filled with strong, scraggly weeds and wildflowers. Just beyond the shop is Mrs. Jimez's news shop. As I pass the shop, rows of apartments line the street. In the distance, I can see two towering office buildings.

WRITE

Ask students to write a story-opener paragraph that describes the story setting. As a first step, have the class brainstorm a list of possibilities and write them on the chalkboard. Examples:

- a forest
- a ballpark
- a fairground
- a deserted building
- a mountain top
- a beach
- a shopping mall
- a subway station
- an airport

Next, list and review a few criteria that can help students as they write and then conference:

1. Imagine that you are in this setting. Choose a focus—near-to-far or far-to-near—and stick to it.
2. Use words and phrases that appeal to the senses.
3. Use metaphors, simile, and personification to build visual images.

One way for partners to start the conference stage is to employ the visual-trip technique. As the writer reads the paragraph aloud, the partner listens to the description with eyes closed, then comments on what he or she saw while listening.

Encourage students to continue with their stories or to file the paragraph in their Writing Folders as a story-starter for the future.

ORGANIZING WITH TIME-ORDER WORDS

Through this activity, students practice using time-order words in describing a series of actions.

What You'll Need
Copies of the reproducible on page 47.

Procedure
1. Ahead of time, write the following paragraph on the chalkboard, providing blanks as shown. Distribute the reproducible. As students study the paragraph together, ask them to find words in the list at the top of the reproducible that make the sequence of events in the paragraph clearer. Write students' responses in the blanks. Various responses are possible, but discourage repetition. (Examples are given in parentheses above the blanks.)

_____(As)_____ I waded through the knee-high grass, I saw a hawk circling above. _____(For a moment)_____, it disappeared behind a distant clump of trees, _____(then)_____ swerved upward again like a kite that had broken free of its string. _____(Just as)_____ I was marveling at its flight, the hawk plunged to the ground and captured a field mouse. I _____(last)_____ caught sight of the great bird as it arched upward _____(until)_____ it was only a sunny flash against the crystal-blue air.

After students have read the completed paragraph, ask them to point out other precise words and images in the paragraph. Review visual focus. Where is the narrator standing? (in a field) What is the general focus? (up-and-down)

2. Ask partners to carry out the assignment described on the reproducible. Encourage them to read their finished paragraph aloud to a group of classmates and ask the audience what they liked best about it.

WRITE

Suggest that students review the story-setting paragraph they wrote for page 37, and continue with another paragraph that tells about an event or series of actions that takes place in that setting, using time-order words to make the sequence clear.

DESCRIBING PEOPLE

Students' descriptions of people tend to be simply a catalogue of physical traits and personal characteristics. Through this activity, students learn how to focus on a particular quality of an individual and organize a description around that focus.

Procedure

1. On the chalkboard, list eight or ten characters from books and stories your students have read. Include characters from nonfiction books, outstanding minor characters as well as major ones, and villains as well as heroes.

Challenge students to come up with one descriptive word or phrase that sums up a major quality of each character. Chart students' ideas next to each character's name. Keep the activity moving fast: first reactions are the most powerful ones here. Examples:

CHARACTER	MAJOR CHARACTERISTIC
Matt (*My Brother Sam Is Dead*)	confused
Orville Wright	determined
Billy Wind (*The Talking Earth*)	courageous
Gretel ("Hansel and Gretel")	clever
Roderick Usher ("The Fall of the House of Usher")	depressed and secretive

2. Ask the class to choose one of the characters and develop together a descriptive paragraph that *shows* the character *acting* in a typical way. Guidelines:

- *Don't tell* what the character is like. That is, don't use the characteristic word from the chart to simply tell the reader that "Gretel was clever" or that "Roderick Usher was depressed."
- *Do show* the person in action, behaving in his or her special, characteristic way.
- Use imagery and vivid sensory words to develop the special characteristic.

You may wish to present and discuss the following example before the class begins to write. How does the paragraph show that the character is depressed? (through visual imagery)

> Roderick Usher moved gloomily around the dimly-lit room. His face drooped with fatigue as he glanced warily at the dark corners. He sighed as if all hope had left him, but otherwise he remained silent as the grave.

You may want to repeat this class practice, using another character from the chart, before students move on to the WRITE activity.

WRITE

For the WRITEs on pages 37 and 38, students created a paragraph that describes a story setting and a paragraph that describes a series of actions. Ask students to read over these paragraphs, then write a third. This paragraph should describe a character, showing—not telling about—one of the person's major characteristics. Talk with students about their options: The paragraph need not be related at all to the first two; however, many students will want to tie it in, because they sense a short story developing.

After students draft their paragraphs, suggest they work with a writing partner.

ORGANIZING PARAGRAPHS OF CONVERSATION

Like Alice in *Alice In Wonderland*, most young people like stories "with conversations in them"; consequently, they like to put conversations into their own stories. You've probably noted, however, that many young writers come up with dialogue that doesn't go anywhere. Example:

"Hi!" said Luis.

"Hi!" said Tio.

Shana came along and said, "Hi! What are you doing?"

Through the following activity, students practice incorporating the descriptive techniques they've learned so far into dialogue that does go somewhere.

What You'll Need
Copies of the reproducible on page 48

Procedure
1. Ahead of time, copy the following chart onto the chalkboard. Leave the last column blank. (Through Step 3 discussion, students will fill in the last column. Many responses are possible. Sample responses during Step 3 are given in parentheses.)

SETTING	SITUATION	CHARACTERS AND WHAT THEY'RE LIKE	WHAT THEY DO: *ACTION*	WHAT THEY SAY: *DIALOGUE*
Playground	The school bully approaches Lena and Hester while they're eating lunch	• **Bully**: gross and mean and full of himself	Grabs Lena's lunch pack	("Gimme that, you squirt!")
		• **Lena**: shy; scared	Hands lunch to bully	(Nothing)
		• **Hester**: protective; brave	Grabs lunch back	("Get out of here, you! Leave her alone!")
City sidewalk	An elderly man has fallen down, and seems to be seriously injured.	• **Shana**: excitable; nervous	Wrings her hands; runs up and down the side-walk	("Help! Someone help!")
		• **Dan**: calm in emergencies	Runs to phone booth	("I'm going to call 911!")
		• **Elderly Man**: in pain; confused	Grips a leg; looks at Shana and Dan	(Just groans and sighs)

2. Present the chart as the beginnings of two writers' story plans. Briefly call attention to the **settings** and **situations** the writers have decided upon. Then have students hunker down into a study of what the characters in each story are **like** (Column 3) and what their **actions** are (Column 4). For each story plan, ask: How are the characters different from one another? How do their actions reflect their personalities and/or the situation in which they find themselves? For example: Why does Lena hand her lunch over to the bully? (She's shy, and she's scared of him.) Why does Dan, not Shana, go to the phone to call 911? (Dan is calm in emergencies; Shana is excitable and nervous.)

3. Ask students to brainstorm for what the different characters might **say** in the situation presented and in view of their personalities. Enter students' ideas in Column 5 and punctuate contributions as dialogue (as shown in parentheses).

4. Review with students:
- In stories, writers try to present characters who are different from one another in important ways. For example, Hester is brave, and Lena is scared. Shana is excitable, and Dan is calm.
- Different characters **act** and **speak** in different ways.
- The different **actions** and **words** of the characters move the story along.

5. Show students how their contributions to the last column on the chart, **dialogue**, can be worked into conversations that move the story along. Example:

> While Lena and Hester were enjoying their lunch on the playground, the bully approached them, looking mean as usual.
> "Gimme that, you squirt!" said the bully, grabbing Lena's lunch pack.
> Lena's scared eyes flickered shyly. Without a word, she handed over her lunch.
> Hester's eyes flashed. "Get out of here," she yelled at the bully, grabbing the lunch back. "Leave her alone!"

6. Distribute the reproducible, which is an adaptation of the chart drawn on the chalkboard in Step 1. Ask students to work independently or with a partner to use the chart to plan a story opener. Encourage students to use their plans to draft some paragraphs of dialogue. If you wish, you might at this point review, using your language arts textbook, the conventions for writing dialogue.

WRITE

Students who have been developing a story using the WRITE activities on pages 37, 38, and 39 may wish to add a fourth section. Suggest that they introduce a second character, different in many ways from the main one, and create a dialogue between these characters. With writing partners, students can read the dialogue aloud to see whether it shows two quite different people reacting in two quite different ways.

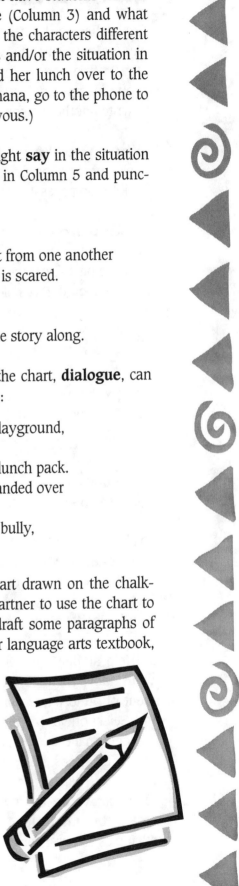

ESTABLISHING ATMOSPHERE IN DESCRIPTIVE PARAGRAPHS

Atmosphere is the general feeling or mood created through a piece of writing. For example, we may say that a description has a somber atmosphere, or a happy, exciting, or angry atmosphere. Through the following activity, students use what they've learned about imagery and precise wording to establish atmosphere in their descriptive paragraphs to write another personal sketch.

What You'll Need
Copies of the reproducible on page 49. Students will also need their copies of the reproducibles on pages 17, 31, and 32

Procedure
1. In a quick oral go-around, ask students to name various moods they've experienced over the past few days and the events that brought these moods about. List responses on the chalkboard. Examples:

Mood	Event
Cheerful	My report card was the best ever.
Angry	Our school's Field Day got rained out.
Expectant Curious	I wondered what was in that big package labeled Do Not Open Until Your Birthday.
Bored	I got tired of watching re-runs on TV.
Excited	My favorite aunt was coming to visit.
Amazed Surprised	My grandfather told me he couldn't speak English until he was 12 years old.

Explain that writers can make their descriptive paragraphs have a "mood," and that the mood of a piece of writing is called its atmosphere. Ask students to recall, from the activities they've carried out previously, some ways writers create atmosphere (imagery, metaphors, precise words, etc.). Have students refer to the reproducibles (see **What You'll Need**) to find examples.

2. Help students develop a strategy that will enable them to make the establishment of atmosphere part of their pre-writing. Select one of the moods from the chart students made in Step 1 above. Enter the mood, or atmosphere, at the center of an idea web. Then ask the class to brainstorm for vivid words and phrases that help to create the atmosphere. Garner as many examples as possible.

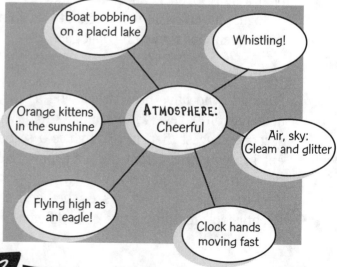

3. Distribute the reproducible on page 49. Have students use it as they work in small groups to draft a paragraph that establishes an atmosphere. Steps for the group to follow:

• Decide on an **event** or a **setting**—real or imaginary—that you want to describe in a paragraph.

• Decide on the **atmosphere** you want to establish in your paragraph. Brainstorm together for vivid words and phrases that may help to create the atmosphere. Write your ideas in the web.

• Together, draft a descriptive paragraph about the event or setting. A group spokesperson will read this paragraph aloud to the class, so you may want to make a second draft for that purpose.

While listening to the groups' paragraphs, the audience should determine what the atmosphere is and what words and phrases create the atmosphere. Some groups may wish to revise their paragraphs based on feedback from classmates. To publish their paragraphs, groups can make a final copy, illustrate the event or setting, and display their work.

WRITE

Suggest that students work independently to write a personal sketch based on a recollection from their own lives, a place whose atmosphere they remember vividly, or an event that evoked strong feelings. Remind students to use the descriptive writing techniques they're learned:

• Choose a visual focus and stick to it.
• Use time-order words to connect events in sequence.
• Show, don't tell. Use imagery and precise, vivid words to create the atmosphere.

It's up to students whether they wish to share this personal sketch with a writing partner at this time. Make sure students file their personal sketches in their Writing Folders, for the sketches will come in handy as students plan their personal essays in Part Four of this book.

ADDITIONAL ACTIVITIES

1. Describing Stage Settings

Students who have been writing plays or reading play scripts are probably familiar with the description of setting that precedes each act. Your writers can use position words and other descriptive words and phrases as they have fun imagining and describing simple or elaborate settings for plays they would like to present.

For this activity, explain that setting is usually described from the viewpoint of the actors as they enter and move about on the stage, not from the viewpoint of the audience. For example, at stage left, a large couch means that the couch is on the actors' left. A good way to demonstrate this "mirror image" is to ask a student to stand in front of the classroom and describe what he or she sees—left, right, and middle—from her or his vantage point facing the class.

Students may wish to talk with partners about a story they'd like to present in play form, then brainstorm for how the stage might be set up for Act One. Remind students that precise position words and descriptive phrases are of great importance to the stagehands who must design and position items in the set. Provide an example:

Cinderella / Act I
Setting: A large kitchen in an old house. At stage left is a door opening to the rest of the house. At stage right is a door opening to the outside. At the center of the stage is a stone fireplace, where a fire burns brightly. A coal scuttle, two brooms, and a mop are against the hearth. A kettle hangs over the fire. To the left of the hearth is a rickety rocking chair in which Cinderella is sitting as the act opens. The whole stage is lit dimly, with only the fire casting a strong, golden glow.

Discuss the example with students. Point out how the description of the setting sets the atmosphere for the first part of the story-play. After they write and share their own Act One settings, students may wish to go ahead and write settings for second and third acts.

2. Haikus About Time
Introduce or review with students the structure of a haiku:

> **First line:** five syllables
> **Second line:** seven syllables
> **Third line:** five syllables

Ask students to write a haiku that describes an event in sequence. Provide examples:

> First, gold sun rising.
> At noon, clouds hover on hills.
> At night, the storm breaks.
>
> Geese fly in moonlight.
> Soon, frogs croak in moonlit ponds.
> Now the spring moon smiles!

As students read their haikus aloud, ask the audience to imagine the events that are unfolding in time order. What words or images provide time clues?

3. When Book Characters Meet
For this activity, students will need to review what they learned using *Organizing Paragraphs of Conversation*, page 48.

Ask students to choose the main characters from two different books they've read, then write a conversation these characters might have if they met one another in one of the following situations:

• A hurricane or other major storm is bearing down on your community.

- A serious argument is brewing between two students in your school.
- A villain threatens to cut off all telephone and Internet communications in your community.

Invite students to read the dialogue aloud with a partner. Ask the audience to listen to see whether the following criteria are fulfilled:
- The dialogue shows how the characters are alike and different.
- The paragraphs include actions that the characters perform.
- The paragraphs move the event long.

4. New Looks at Old Fables

On the chalkboard, list some morals from traditional fables with which your students are familiar. Ask students to choose one of the morals and create a new fable that teaches the same lesson. As a prewriting strategy, review and list any descriptive writing techniques you want students to especially attend to and practice. Examples:
- Organize with time-order words.
- *Show* your characters in action.
- Make sure any dialogue moves the story along and reveals something about the characters' personalities.

Some Famous Morals

- Slow and steady wins the race.
- Don't count your chickens before they're hatched.
- It is easy to despise what one cannot have.
- Liars will not be believed, even when they tell the truth.
- Your acts of kindness will always come back to you.
- Beware of the wolf in sheep's clothing.

5. Unusual Recipes and Directions

Invite students to write "recipes" for making things, situations, atmospheres, and events like the following:

- a thunderstorm
- a traffic jam
- a snowflake
- laughter
- friendship
- confusion
- gloom
- night

Set up some guidelines:
- Use time-order.
- Use precise words to describe each step exactly.
- Use imagery and sensory words to make your recipe fun to read.

Students can bind their work in a class Recipe Book and/or make copies of some of the recipes to share with families at home.

POSITION WORDS

Use these lists for reference as you organize your descriptive paragraphs.

Top to Bottom, Bottom to Top, Side to Side

above	behind	in front of
across from	below	inside
against	beneath	leading to
along side of	beside	middle
at the base of	close to	near
at the bottom of	down	next to
at the left	halfway	top
at the right	in back of	under, underneath
	over	up
		upon

Near to Far, Far to Near

above	beside	midway
ahead	beyond	near
around	close	next to
at a distance	far away	outside
away from	forward	top
behind	halfway	toward
beneath	inside	

TIME-ORDER WORDS

Use this list for reference as you organize your descriptive paragraphs.

after	earlier	last
afterward	finally	later
as	first	meanwhile
at the same time	for a moment	next
before	immediately	soon
before long	instantly	then
	just as	until

Activity:

With a partner, write a paragraph about an exciting event, real or fictional.
You can use one of the titles below as an idea or choose a title and idea
of your own. Guidelines:

- Use time-order words to help readers follow the action.
- Use sensory words and metaphors to help readers see the action.
- Do not write a paragraph about a dream!

Titles and Ideas

- The Bear in the Tree
- Emergency Landing
- The Terrible Picnic
- The Wrong Shoe
- The Happiest Day
- Lost on the Fairgrounds
- A Noise in the Basement
- Now, Where Did That Cat Go!
- Big Storm
- Running with the Wind

_____

_____

_____

_____

_____

_____

_____

Name _____

ORGANIZING PARAGRAPHS OF CONVERSATION

Use the chart below to plan a story opener.

Setting of My Story: _____

_____

_____

Here's the situation as the story opens: _____

_____

_____

_____

_____

Characters' Names and What They're Like	What the Characters Do: ACTION	What the Characters Say: DIALOGUE
1.		
2.		
3.		

AN ATMOSPHERE WEB

Event or Setting We Will Describe: _____
_____
_____

ATMOSPHERE:

_____

_____

_____

PART FOUR

DESCRIPTIVE WRITING EVERY DAY AND ACROSS THE CURRICULUM

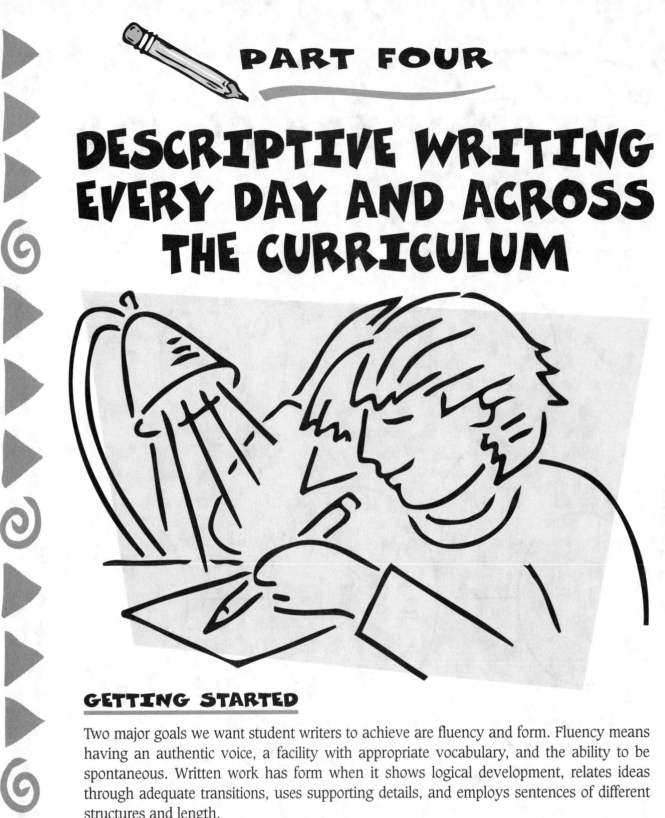

GETTING STARTED

Two major goals we want student writers to achieve are fluency and form. Fluency means having an authentic voice, a facility with appropriate vocabulary, and the ability to be spontaneous. Written work has form when it shows logical development, relates ideas through adequate transitions, uses supporting details, and employs sentences of different structures and length.

The only way for students to achieve fluency and form is to write often, preferably every day and for different purposes. Fortunately, descriptive writing techniques can be applied to writing in every subject area. When you show students how to use these techniques as a natural part of all their writing, their fluency and form will grow, and so will their grasp of all the concepts and skills you are teaching, across the curriculum.

DESCRIPTIVE WRITING WARM-UPS

There are several advantages to carrying out a brief morning warm-up three or four times a week according to the following procedure.

✔ **Students** get lots of writing practice within a short time, receive immediate feedback, and learn writing techniques by listening to their peers' work. In addition, because students know they're writing for an audience of classmates, and because they don't know ahead of time whether *their* paragraph will be the one chosen for oral reading, they tend to put special effort into their writing.

✔ **Teachers** don't have to evaluate entire sets of papers every day. At the same time, the activity allows teachers to make regular assessments of students' development in descriptive writing.

Procedure

1. Write a "starter statement" on the chalkboard. Point out that the statement is a *telling* sentence. Students are not to use the statement in their paragraph. Instead, the paragraph should develop the idea by *showing*, that is, by using descriptive writing strategies. Examples of starter sentences:

- The old man was sad.
- The room was dark and dusty.
- The two friends were angry at one another.

(Note: A starter sentence works better than a "topic"—for example, *Sadness*, *A Room*, *Friendship*—in this warm-up context because the sentence presents a controlling idea and thus gets kids writing more quickly.)

Make the writing activity a *timed* one. As students grow in fluency, ten minutes is enough for drafting the paragraph.

2. Collect the paragraphs. Select four or five of them to read aloud to the class. Ask students to comment on the details and content of the paragraphs (*not* on grammar). On the students' papers that you've read aloud, write a helpful summary of the class reaction and enter your own reaction into the student's Writing Assessment Record. Examples of class-reaction summaries:

- We like the vivid metaphors. We thought some of the details didn't belong. Your paragraph has great action words.
- The part we like best is the description of anger. We wish your paragraph had more conversation.

3. Return all the paragraphs for students to file in their Writing Folders. Some students may wish to revise their paragraphs. With students who are disappointed that you didn't read *their* paragraphs aloud, schedule brief one-on-one reading sessions over the next couple of days.

DESCRIPTIVE WRITING ABOUT SCIENCE AND TECHNOLOGY

While "science writing" is basically expository, the use of descriptive writing techniques makes the writing vivid and precise. You can help students accept and enjoy writing as a natural follow-up to observations, procedures, and conclusions related to their science activities.

Procedure

1. Have each student organize and regularly write in a Science Journal. The Journal can be divided into two sections:

- Regular step-by-step entries recording structured investigations conducted with the class as a whole or with a small group of classmates
- On-your-own paragraphs about events and phenomena the student has observed or read about independently

2. Present the following draft and revision and discuss how descriptive writing techniques enhance a science report:

The Draft:

ROCKS

We collected rocks and stones. The rocks had different shapes and textures. We wanted to find out some things about them. The first thing we wanted to do was find out what's inside. We wrapped one stone and hit it. The stone was different colors inside. Another stone had a fossil inside it.

The Revision:

ROCK HISTORIES AND MYSTERIES

Our geology group collected ten different rocks and stones. Some of the rocks were smooth and almost silky, while others were jagged and rough. The first thing we wanted to discover was what was inside the rocks. We wrapped one of the roughest stones in a cloth and hit it with a hammer. We were amazed to see streaks of purple, blue, and red inside the stone. What would we find inside another stone? We struck it with the hammer, and as the stone crumbled in two we saw the impression of a leaf that had fallen to earth thousands of years ago.

3. Have students brainstorm for a chalkboard list of familiar science and technology subjects that they could describe. Example:

Describe:
- The relationship between living things in a woods or park nearby
- How a clock works
- How birds use their beaks and feet
- How a battery, bulb, and wire make a system that will light a flashlight
- How condensation happens on a cold surface
- The metamorphosis of a butterfly
- How Curie (or Newton, Copernicus, Einstein) have affected scientists today
- What happens during a solar eclipse
- What causes ocean tides (volcanic eruptions, earthquakes, hurricanes, tornadoes, etc.)
- How an airplane flies

Ask the class to choose an item from the chalkboard list and compose together a paragraph about it that is rich in describing words and phrases.

WRITE

Ask students to begin the On-Your Own section of their science/technology journals by writing about a phenomenon they can readily describe through observation or investigation. Examples:

- weather
- star-sightings and formations
- how a compass works
- how a remote-control works

- their own energy levels
- how pets indicate their needs
- how food creates energy
- traffic patterns

Establish some simple criteria and ask partners to use the criteria as they share and discuss their work.

- The steps follow a time-sequence.
- All the main steps are provided.
- Descriptive words and phrases make the steps clear and interesting to the reader.

THOSE SPELLING LISTS!

The words students are asked to master can be the imaginative spurs for independent descriptive writing.

Procedure

1. List the spelling words on the chalkboard. On the chalkboard or on an overhead projector, show these two ways (see page 54) in which the words can be used in a description:

• general	• haughty	• enormous	• Tuesday	• yacht
• laboratory	• autumn	• quiet	• loud	

On a brisk <u>autumn</u> day, <u>General</u> Fluppsy secretly boarded his <u>enormous yacht</u>. On this <u>Tuesday</u>, he would test his secret <u>laboratory</u>. <u>Loud</u> thunder clouds boomed on the horizon. "<u>Quiet!</u>" yelled the General, in his usual <u>haughty</u> way.

There was an <u>enormous</u> feeling of <u>quiet</u> on <u>Tuesday</u> as we listened to Tim tell about his trip last <u>autumn</u> aboard a <u>yacht</u>. In a <u>loud</u> and <u>haughty</u> voice, Tim let us know that the yacht was a <u>laboratory</u> ship, not just a pleasure craft.

2. After discussing how the spelling-list words are used in the examples to create different situations and imagery, ask the class to use the words to compose a group paragraph presenting another scenario. As the class presents each spelling word orally, ask a student to come to the chalkboard and write the word correctly into the evolving paragraph.

WRITE

Encourage students to use the words from each week's spelling list in descriptive paragraphs of their own. From time to time, invite students to read their paragraphs aloud. Ask the audience to respond with ideas about how to extend the paragraphs into short stories.

A MATH DESCRIBE-IT-TO-ME

Students can use what they discover about area and size to describe how to measure, figure, and repeat an operation.

What You'll Need
A bedspread for a double bed; if possible, some pictures of patchwork quilts from art books on the subject

Procedure
1. On the chalkboard, draw the outline of patchwork quilt: six patches across and eight rows from top to bottom. If you're also using pictures of patchwork quilts, have students discuss the patterns and themes they detect in the quilts. Discuss quilting bees, how each patch is of the same size, and how quilters figure the sizes of the patches they'll make. "Figuring" will involve students in measuring the length and width of the bedspread and then deciding on the dimensions of each of the 48 squares.

2. Pose various word problems involving the quilt. Examples:

- There are six (four, eight, two) quiltmakers, and each one will make an equal number of patches. How many patches will each quilter make? (8, 12, 6, 24)
- The quilt will show an equal number of flowers, trees, and houses. How many of each will be shown on the quilt? (16)
- One quiltmaker wants to make the quilt one patch wider and one patch longer. How many extra patches will this quiltmaker have to make? (14: 6 across + 8 down)

3. Have students work with a partner to plan and draw a patchwork quilt. The design should include:

- An overall drawing of the quilt
- An even number of squares
- The same dimensions for each square
- A repeated design
- Repeated colors for the design

Ask partners to use the bedspread, rulers, and tape measures as they plan and design their quilt. Partners should make notes each step of the way to show what they did in that step.

WRITE

Using their notes, partners write a step-by-step description of how to make their quilt. They read their steps as they show the quilt pattern to classmates. The audience gives feedback about what is clear and what is not. Partners revise on the basis of classmates' input.

Ask partners to make final drawings of their quilts and final copies of the descriptive directions for making them. Display students' work.

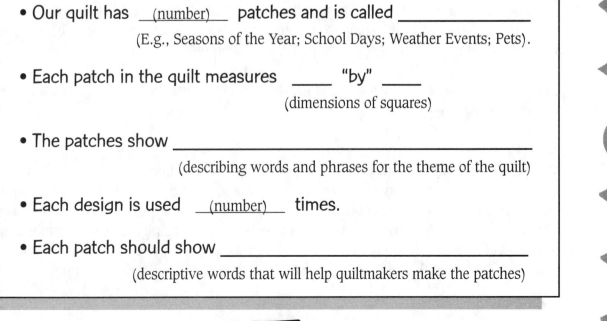

- Our quilt has ___(number)___ patches and is called _____
  (E.g., Seasons of the Year; School Days; Weather Events; Pets).

- Each patch in the quilt measures _____ "by" _____
  (dimensions of squares)

- The patches show _____
  (describing words and phrases for the theme of the quilt)

- Each design is used ___(number)___ times.

- Each patch should show _____
  (descriptive words that will help quiltmakers make the patches)

HISTORY: JOURNEYS BACK IN TIME

Visual trips into the past help students understand how people fared long ago and engender images that students can use in describing historical events and situations.

Procedure

1. To help students see a pioneer home 150 years ago, ask them to close their eyes and imagine these contrasting scenes as you describe them:

> Imagine your own home. See the refrigerator, the stove, the TV set. Hear the radio inside, and the sounds of cars and trucks outside. Feel the heat coming up through the radiators. Touch the warmth of blankets. Open the windows to catch a cool breeze. Taste the yummyness of the burger or pizza you've just bought at the store down the block or that you've heated up quickly in your oven or microwave. Now you're turning on a light so that you can finish that great book you're reading. Oops! The telephone rings. You answer and have a fine conversation with a friend who lives many miles away.

> Now imagine yourself in a home where there is no electric stove, no refrigerator, no telephone, no TV or radio, no radiators, no electric lights. Take away all those things from your mental picture. Outside it is silent. There is only one door and one window in your house, and the window is not made to open. A dim fire burns in a small fireplace, and a kettle steams over it, filled with whatever meat and plants you've managed to gather over a hard day's hunting. Soon it will be pitch dark. There will be only candlelight by which to read the one book you have. And though you may be lonely, you have no way of talking with friends in faraway places.

2. After presenting the visual trip, ask the class to recall the details that build mental images. Then have students compose together some descriptive paragraphs about a pioneer family settling down for the night in a rough cabin on the frontier.

Encourage students to use dialogue in their descriptions. Write the class paragraphs on the chalkboard, leaving plenty of space between each line for revision.

WRITE

Whenever time allows, encourage students to imagine themselves as a participant or onlooker in an historical event or era that the class is studying. Ask students to *show* what they see and hear and to describe the feelings they have. Invite your writers to read their descriptions aloud. The strategy gives students an opportunity to react empathetically to historical events and provides you with a way to assess not only students' understanding of the event but also the development of their skills in descriptive writing.

SENTENCE-WRITING SKILLS

Writing sentences is more than a mechanical grammatical skill. Present sentence structure and sentence combining in its real-life, writerly context: to make descriptions more compelling and effective. There are two basic strategies for students to experiment with in this context. One is to combine sentences to stress major images. The other is to write sentences that reflect the pace of the actions the writer is describing.

Procedure

1. On the chalkboard, present pairs of sentences and ask students to identify the vivid descriptive words and phrases in each sentence. Underline students' choices. Examples:

- <u>Wild</u> water <u>gushed</u> under the <u>fragile</u> bridge.
- The bridge <u>swayed</u>.

- A <u>frightened</u> dog <u>snarled</u> and <u>bolted into the underbrush</u>.
- The dog was <u>skinny</u> and <u>coated with mud</u>.

- George and Selena <u>clung desperately to the drifting raft</u>.
- The raft <u>hurtled through the rapids</u>.

2. Ask the class to combine the images in each pair into a single sentence. There will be various ways to do this; record them on the chalkboard. Examples:

- Wild water gushed under the fragile, swaying bridge.
- The fragile bridge swayed as the wild water gushed under it.

- The skinny dog, snarling, frightened, and coated with mud, bolted into the underbrush.
- The frightened, skinny, snarling, mud-coated dog bolted into the underbrush.

- George and Selena clung desperately to the drifting raft as it hurtled through the rapids.
- As the drifting raft hurtled through the rapids, George and Selena clung desperately to it.

Young writers like to hear that their sentences sound "grown-up." So, in discussing students' sentence combinations and reading them aloud, stress the professional, "grown-up," writerly sound that the images attain through combining the sentences.

3. Write the following topics on the chalkboard. Discuss with students which topics suggest abrupt, short movements and which suggest ongoing, flowing movements.

(Abrupt, short)
- A car that has engine problems
- Moving chess figures on a chessboard
- Playing hopscotch

(On-going, flowing)
- Swimming in a gentle ocean
- Leaves drifting down from autumn trees
- Listening to calm music

4. After students have correctly categorized the examples in **Step 3**, present on the chalkboard examples of how sentence length can capture the movement the writer is describing.

(Abrupt, short movement)
- The car choked. Gushes of steam poured out. Rattles rumbled from the engine. Gassy odors wafted over me.

(On-going, flowing movement)
- The soft water held me as I floated sleepily on its surface, lapped in the lullaby whisper of gentle waves.

Ask partners to choose another of the examples from the chalkboard list and write a descriptive sentence or sentences that capture the movement and pace of the event. As students read their sentences aloud, ask the audience to listen to determine how sentence length contributes to the image of the event.

WRITE

In a brainstorm session, have students name for a chalkboard list some recent events or situations they've experienced in school or at home. Examples:

- A power outage! All the electricity turned off.
- Stray dog (cat) at the door. We argue about whether or not to take it in and feed it.
- I did my homework, but I actually, really, truly lost it before I got to school!
- Chores at home. Who does what? How do we decide?
- Baby-sitting. Good experiences and bad ones.
- Everybody in my reading group except me really likes (doesn't like) the book we're reading.

Ask students to write independently on one of the topics the class has brainstormed. Review the writing-activity guidelines for writers and their partners:

- Adjust sentence length to capture the movement and action you're describing.
- Combine descriptive words and phrases to make your sentences sound grown-up and writerly.

CULMINATING ACTIVITY: WRITING A PERSONAL ESSAY

Most students will need four or five writing periods to plan, draft, and revise their personal essays.

What You'll Need
Copies of the reproducible on page 63; a copy of the model essay, page 64 to show on the overhead projector

Procedure
1. **Session One:** *Prewrite*. Write the following definition on the chalkboard:

Personal Essay:
   ✔ A short composition...
   ✔ ...on a single subject..
   ✔ ...presenting the author's personal views and impressions.

To point out to students that they already have the skills to write a personal essay, show how the definition applies.

- Your essay will have three paragraphs.
- Look through your writing folders to find a subject to write about.
- Use descriptive words and phrases to make your views and impressions vivid and clear.

Show the model. Discuss with students how it fulfills the criteria for a personal essay. Then distribute the reproducible. Preview the procedure, then ask students to refer to their writing folders to: **A.** Select a single subject for their essays and to draft a topic sentence that states the main idea they will develop. (Remind students that the topic sentence can always be revised later on.) **B.** Brainstorm independently for several descriptive words and phrases they could use to develop the idea.

2. **Session Two:** *Draft.* Ask students to write a first draft of paragraphs one and two of their personal essays. Whether using a word processor or pencil and paper, students should leave plenty of space between the lines of their draft.

3. Session Three: Before students draft the third and final paragraph of their essays, suggest that they conference with a writing partner, using these steps:

- Read the draft of the first two paragraphs aloud to your partner. As you read, you may wish to make your own notes about details you'd like to add.
- Ask your partner to comment on your draft.
- Use the Say-Back strategy. Ask your partner:
    - ✔ Say-back to me the atmosphere you sense in my paragraphs.
    - ✔ Say-back to me the main feeling or emotion you sense that I, the writer, have in these paragraphs.
    - ✔ Say-back to me in your own words what the main idea is that I'm developing.
- Use what you've discovered through your partner conference to draft the last paragraph of your personal essay.

(Note: Say-backs are valuable to writers because they serve as checks to ascertain whether the intended message and mood are coming across to readers, and because they provide the writer with his or her own additional ideas about how to conclude the essay in paragraph three.)

4. Session Four: *Revise.* Ask students to read and re-read the drafts of their personal essays. Present some revision guidelines:

- Change or add imagery to build sensory impressions. Delete ideas that don't belong.
- Make sure your sentences follow a time-order or stick to a spatial focus.
- Give some final thoughts to the central idea of your essay.

Does the topic sentence in the first paragraph accurately state your main idea? Does the last paragraph state this idea in a different way and show how all the details in the essay support it?

Many students—especially the crackerjack writers!—may want a fifth session in which to polish their personal essays.

5. Have students brainstorm for ways to publish their personal essays. In addition to reading them aloud to classmates and taking copies home to share with families, students can bind all the essays into an anthology. Students can volunteer to create these features of the anthology:

- **A Book Jacket Design**
Design a picture. Write a title for the anthology and letter it in an eye-catching way.

- **Book Jacket Copy**

For the inside flaps, write highlights or main ideas of some of the personal essays. For the back of the jacket, write "rave reviews" of the anthology.

- **A Table of Contents**
- **An Introduction**

You may wish to brainstorm with students about this feature. Point out that an Introduction can tell how the project (writing personal essays) began; what the writers learned from the experience; why readers will enjoy the anthology.

ADDITIONAL ACTIVITIES

1. Completing or Starting Short Stories

Encourage students who have been building a short story by using the activities in Parts One, Two, and Three to finish their stories. For students who have yet to get going on this project, review and provide some start-up steps:

- Select a place and write a telling sentence about it. Examples:
  The school was empty.
  The fairground was noisy.
  The ocean was rough.

Now write a paragraph showing the place. Do not use your telling sentence in your paragraph.

- Select two characters. Write two telling sentences to identify them. Examples:
  She was a veterinarian.
  He was a firefighter.

Now write a paragraph showing what these characters are like and what they're doing in your setting. Do not use your telling sentences.

- Write dialogue for your two characters. The conversation should reflect their personalities and show how they're different.
- Write a paragraph describing the conflict the characters are having or the problem they are trying to solve.
- In the rest of your story, show how the conflict or problem is solved.

2. Post Offices and Mailbags: Letters from the Past

Ask students to list several characters from a fiction book or persons from history who interacted in an event. Have students imagine letters that these people might have sent to relatives or friends, describing key situations and actions in which they were involved. Remind students that the purpose of the letters is to help the recipients see and imagine the situation in their mind's eye.

3. Let's Advertise!

Students can write highly descriptive copy for display ads, catalogues, or TV or radio commercials. As students probably know, these advertisements use imagery and strong descriptive phrases to urge the reading or listening audience to buy some particular goods or services. While students might write copy for something that's actually desirable and popular, a more challenging variation is to write copy meant to sell something a bit unusual. Examples:

- mail-order snowballs
- banana peels
- shoes for dogs
- socks that don't match
- skunk perfume
- used matches

4. My Diary of the Future

Ask students to imagine themselves 20 years from now, engaged in an exciting situation or event, and writing a diary entry about it. To provide a focus, students can write a telling sentence about the event. For example:

- I've been selected to travel on a space shuttle to the moon.
- I just won a million dollars in a lottery.
- The book I wrote (building I designed; cure I discovered; movie I starred in, etc.) has been honored with an international prize.

The diary entry should not use the telling sentence but should develop the idea through descriptive strategies.

5. Tall Tales

Tall tales, with their exaggerations and grandiose descriptions, are a natural form for students to use as they apply what they know about descriptive writing. Students can write the further adventures of tall-tale heroines and heroes they've already read about or create original characters and set the tales in modern times.

PLANNING A PERSONAL ESSAY

1. Main idea of my essay:

_____

_____

A draft of my topic sentence:

_____

_____

Some descriptive words and phrases I might use:

_____

_____

_____

2. Three supporting ideas for my first paragraph:

_____

_____

_____

Some images and details for my second paragraph:

_____

_____

_____

3. Conference notes: What is the *atmosphere* of my paragraph?

_____

_____

_____

How can I strengthen the first two paragraphs?

_____

_____

_____

4. Draft the last paragraph of your essay. Show how all the details and images you've used support your main idea.

MODEL ESSAY

TITLE AND FIRST SENTENCE: *establish* the main idea.

SUPPORT THE MAIN IDEA: an *extraordinary* friend!

BUILD THE MAIN IDEA: examples and images

RESTATE THE MAIN IDEA: an extraordinary friend affected your life—show how details prove it

The Best Friend

Some friends are so extraordinary that they affect your life forever. I know, because many long years ago my life was affected by a tiny, green, elf-like fellow named Deegan Baby. Deegan Baby lived on the radiator cover in the kitchen, had long purple hair, and a sly, high laugh, and wore shoes that curled up at the toes. You won't be shocked to learn that Deegan was purely imaginary. He was invisible to everyone but me.

Deegan never scolded me, never snatched things away, and never fibbed. When I was sad, he sang cheery songs or made hilarious faces to make me smile. When I wanted talk, Deegan gave me his total attention. When I wanted to listen, Deegan told me long, involved stories about his pranks, jokes, and adventures.

When I was four years old, my life changed radically. My baby brother was born. Three kids about my age moved into the house next door. Three mornings a week, I went merrily off to nursery school. And Deegan? He simply disappeared and never came back. But he lives in my heart as sharp and clear as a new photo. You see, Deegan taught me how to be a best friend to others: listen, share, and just be there. I try to use those Deegan lessons every day.